Geologic Time Scale

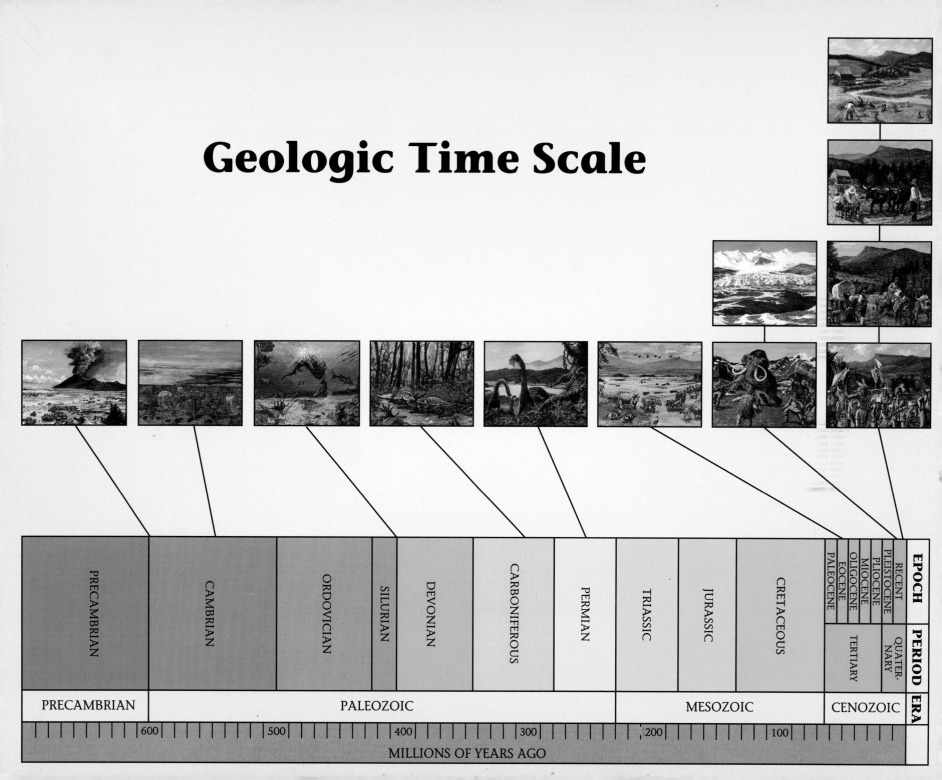

	EPOCH	PERIOD	ERA
PRECAMBRIAN			PRECAMBRIAN
CAMBRIAN			PALEOZOIC
ORDOVICIAN			
SILURIAN			
DEVONIAN			
CARBONIFEROUS			
PERMIAN			
TRIASSIC			MESOZOIC
JURASSIC			
CRETACEOUS			
PALEOCENE / EOCENE / OLIGOCENE / MIOCENE / PLIOCENE		TERTIARY	CENOZOIC
PLEISTOCENE / RECENT		QUATER-NARY	

600 500 400 300 200 100

MILLIONS OF YEARS AGO

I jumped as my mother's voice called me. "Come to breakfast, dear!" Her voice pulled me out of the past and into the present. I tried to think about the day ahead, but my mind was still far away on the things I had seen: the people, the animals, and the plants that had lived so long ago.

Ever since that day, I've looked for bones and fossils that might have been left in that most amazing place: my own backyard.

Then I caught a glimpse of a world so strange that I could hardly believe my eyes. There was a beach with hissing sulphur springs, and the only life was in the form of strange, dome-shaped algae. A volcano belched smoke in the distance. It was hard to believe that this place was my backyard four billion years ago, at the beginning of life on our planet.

Then the waters began to get shallow. The fish disappeared and the plants sank down to mostly green and blue algae. Brown-green, muddy water reflected the light of the sun in a weird, eerie sky. Round jellyfish pulsed by. Some animals that looked like upside-down bowls with legs walked across the muddy bottom past sponges and sea fans.

The view from my window got blurry as the water in the swamp got deeper and deeper. When the land was all underwater, a huge fish with big teeth swam by, chasing two sharks. Around the coral and seaweed, unusual fish wore hard shells.

My wildest dreams were nothing compared to my backyard millions of years ago!

Now, strange, huge trees appeared, and the smell of rotting leaves filled the air. I saw animals that looked like the ancestors of lizards and centipedes. Giant dragonflies skimmed over the surface of the water and the muddy land. The trees had green trunks, but I could not see very far between them because the air was thick with mist.

I watched as once again the years slipped away. Now the trees looked like palms and ferns, and my backyard was swampy and hot.

Huge dinosaurs lived in my backyard, eating tropical plants in the morning haze. They looked like an apatosaurus family. Fantastic birds flew across the sky, which was strangely bright. A baby stegosaurus grazed right in front of my window!

Then the animal and people ran away, and it looked much warmer in my backyard. Tall grasses and giant trees grew in a land of wild beauty, a land where no person had ever walked.

The animals did not look quite like ones I had seen at the zoo. As they came to the brook to drink, I understood that this valley belonged to these creatures.

They looked like distant relatives of camels, giraffes, hippos, monkeys and other animals that no longer live anywhere near my backyard.

Then, in a blink of my eye, the ice was gone. People wearing animal skins were trying to drive away an animal that looked like a big, furry elephant. I saw a frightened family crouching near their fire. They were holding tools made of stone. I could see paintings on a flat rock wall of the shelter where they slept.

Snow began to fall, as if it were winter. Through the swirling blizzard, I sensed that time was moving backward very quickly. A thousand years. Ten thousand years! Back to a time when great ice sheets moved down from the north and covered the land.

When the snow let up, my backyard was covered with blue-white ice, a mile thick at its highest peak. The only sound was of the ice creaking and scraping the rocks and frozen land as the ice moved forward with a mighty weight.

As the settlers rose to leave, a mist blew over the brook. When it cleared, I saw a group of Native Americans. They were lined up to take turns shooting their bows and arrows at a target. In the same spot where our summer barbecue is today, a woman was cooking meat that sizzled over the fire. Newly-picked corn, squash, acorns, and berries made me think that this must be a harvest celebration before the first settlers came from Europe.

Then all at once, right before my eyes, the sawmill disappeared. A covered wagon and a band of settlers were trying to find their way through the river valley that was my backyard.

Their wagon carried food, books, clothes, and iron tools. Their leader was asking a frontiersman about what lay ahead. The settlers were using my backyard as a stopping place as they looked for a place to build a log cabin.

I closed my eyes and shook my head. When I looked again, the farm was gone, and people were using a team of oxen to drag a tree trunk to the building beside the brook. It was an old-fashioned sawmill. Men at the mill were pushing the trunks toward a big saw that cut the wood into boards. Maybe the boards from the sawmill would be used to build houses and barns for the first farmers in the area.

To my surprise, as I looked across my mother's garden toward the brook, my backyard began to look like a farm. People were cutting hay with old-fashioned scythes like I had seen in pictures. Next to the brook was a strange old building with a waterwheel. The hills were plowed fields for growing hay and corn. What I was seeing out my window was my backyard one hundred years ago!

Raising the window shade, I wondered how many other jays had lived in my backyard. Then I wondered how many people had stood where I was, looking at this very same place.

I woke up one morning to the sound of a bluejay squawking outside my bedroom window.

Published by
Charlesbridge Publishing
85 Main Street, Watertown, MA 02472
(617) 926-0329
www.charlesbridge.com

Library of Congress Cataloging-in Publication Data
Kurjian, Judi.
  In my own backyard / by Judi Kurjian; illustrated by
David R. Wagner.
      p.   cm.
  Summary: A young child looks out a bedroom window
seeing the backyard as it would have looked if she had seen
it during various historical and geological periods.
  ISBN 0-88106-442-4 (reinforced for library use)
  ISBN 0-88106-444-0 (softcover)
  [1. Space and time—Fiction. I. Wagner, David, 1940 –   ill.
II. Title   93-18472
PZ7.K956In   1993

Printed in the United States of America
(hc) 10 9 8 7 6 5 4 3 2
(sc) 10 9 8 7 6 5 4 3 2 1
Printed on recycled paper

In My Own Backyard

by **Judi Kurjian**

Illustrated by **David R. Wagner**

 Charlesbridge